Tangled Hair Day

By Jaala Ozies

Library For All Ltd.

Tangled Hair Day

First published 2023

Published by Library For All Ltd
Email: info@libraryforall.org
URL: libraryforall.org

Our Yarning logo design by Jason Lee, Bidjipidji Art

Original illustrations by Margarita Yeromina

Tangled Hair Day
Ozies, Jaala
ISBN: 978-1-922991-13-3
SKU03379

Tangled Hair Day

We respect and honour Aboriginal and Torres Strait Islander Elders past, present and future. We acknowledge the stories, traditions and living cultures of Aboriginal and Torres Strait Islander peoples on this land and commit to building a brighter future together.

I'm brushing my hair, but it keeps getting stuck!

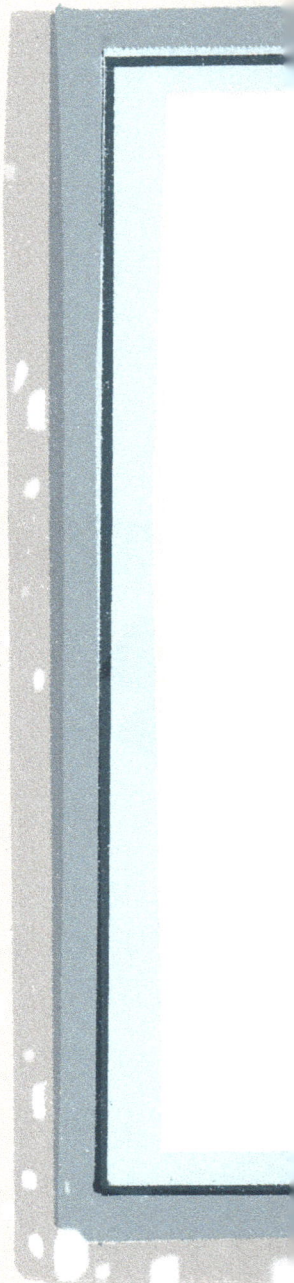

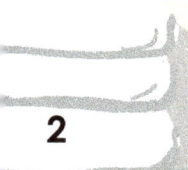

Mum says,
"Let me see if I
have better luck."

"Your hair is very tangled up," she agrees.

Some gubinge hair food
is what you need.

Brush hair starting at the ends with the gubinge hair food.

"Mum, the brush is not pulling my hair anymore and that feels so good."

The hair food makes your hair oily, so the brush can untangle your knots.

Gubinge hair
food helped my
hair lots.

My hair is untangled
and I feel good!

You can use these questions to talk about this book with your family, friends and teachers.

What did you learn from this book?

Describe this book in one word. Funny? Scary? Colourful? Interesting?

How did this book make you feel when you finished reading it?

What was your favourite part of this book?

download our reader app
getlibraryforall.org

About the author

Jaala was born in Perth and now lives in Broome. She is from the Djugun, Karajarri, Nyikina, Kija and Gija Nations. Jaala loves going fishing and camping with her family. Her parents' stories were her favourite when she was a child.

Our Yarning

Want to discover more books from this collection? Our Yarning is a collection of books written by Aboriginal and Torres Strait Islander peoples across Australia.

We know that children learn better, and enjoy reading more, when they see themselves in the stories, characters and illustrations of the books they read.

To download the app, visit the Google Play Store on any Android device and search 'Our Yarning'.

www.ingramcontent.com/pod-product-compliance
Lightning Source LLC
Chambersburg PA
CBHW042350040426
42448CB00031B/3456